EVERLASTING
Verses

EVERLASTING
Verses

NATASA CUC TO

ReadersMagnet, LLC

Everlasting Verses
Copyright © 2023 by Natasa Cuc To

Published in the United States of America
ISBN   Paperback: 978-1-960629-19-7
ISBN   eBook: 978-1-960629-20-3

All rights reserved. No part of this publication may be reproduced, stored in a retrieval system or transmitted in any way by any means, electronic, mechanical, photocopy, recording or otherwise without the prior permission of the author except as provided by USA copyright law.

The opinions expressed by the author are not necessarily those of ReadersMagnet, LLC.

ReadersMagnet, LLC
10620 Treena Street, Suite 230 | San Diego, California, 92131 USA
1.619. 354. 2643 | www.readersmagnet.com

Book design copyright © 2023 by ReadersMagnet, LLC. All rights reserved.

Cover design by Ericka Obando
Interior design by Dorothy Lee

TABLE OF CONTENTS

You And I	11
A Winter Love	12
Our Leaders	13
Friends -	14
That Summer Moment	15
I Dreamed...	16
The Languages	17
Afternoon Autumn's Love	19
The Christmas	20
Loving You	21
Him And Fall	22
You Are...	23
The Red Rose	24
Don't Ask Me	25
Grandma	26
The Morning Love	27
Desire	28
The Lovely Fall	29
Teenager	30
Love You	31
The Kisses	32
Waiting Him	33
The Wedding's Day	34
Only For Him	35
Letter For Dad	36
A Baby Boy	37
His Eyes	38
Missing Love	39

I Wish	40
Love	41
Friend	42
The Happiness Of Life	43
Mom	44
Autumn At Virginia	45
Her	46
Buddha	47
The Bittersweet Love	48
The Dream Lover	49
Love Life	50
Life Goes On	51
The Red Tulip	52
Missing Colors	53
Him	54
Loneliness	55
Fall	56
The Poets	57
The Seductive Evening	58
Spring Fever	59
Loneliness	60
Him And Sunshine	61
In His Hands	62
Our Friendship	63
The Squirrels	64
My Childhood	65
Dad	66
The Lady Moon	67
Unknown Heroes	68
Thich Ca Buddha	69
The High School	70
The Heroes	71

RIVIERA

From the Saigon-born and award-winning poet, Natasa C. To comes the compilation of sensitive poems that springs from the heart. Explore magical times as she takes you through the Everlasting Verses.

Filled with beautiful scenes of people, places, heritage and historical events, paints a picture of deep moments that will move you. Its more mature poems evoke vivid romantic, erotic images of love that will stir your heart's desires. Sometimes subtle, sometimes intensely passionate, To's sensual verses flow with emotion and imagination. Enjoy each emotive piece as it takes you through different paths and experiences!

ABOUT THE AUTHOR

Natasa C. To was born in Saigon. She is an award-winning poet whose works have been published internationally in literary at www.poemhunter.com. She resides with her sisters, Lisa To, Quyen To, her niece Cindy To and her brother Vu To in Gainesville, VA.

FORWARD

Throughout life, I store information collected from an imagination and try in some way to make sense of it. When I am not able to fully understand the things that occur in love lives, I often externalize the information. By doing this, I am afforded a different point of view, thus allowing me to think more clearly about the difficult love life and emotions.

Art is one of the ways in which I choose to express my thoughts "Everlasting Verses" Within the arts, modes of expression differ, but poetry is a very powerful tool by which I can express sometimes delight, sometimes perfectly clear concepts and feelings with events, the love life, two hearts meeting or their making love etc… Intentions can run the feelings as well. I may simply want to share something that touches people's love life or daily activities in some way, or I may want to give help to express the emotion within the poems.

The poetry within "Everlasting Verses" is from every point of view: every topic or emotion imaginable. Some poems will speak to certain readers more than others, but it is always important to keep in mind that each verse is an imagination of a poet, of a mind that need to meet the enjoying and satisfaction of this world poetry, of a heart that feels the effects of every special moment in life, and perhaps of a memory that stirs within the emotion of the readers. Nonetheless, recalling my yesterdays gives joy and happiness to readers in many forms of feelings.

You and I

For the poets who fall in love with each other.

Tenderness of you that touch
tulips memories of spring
Such loving belongs to me
today I still wait for you
as always the love I got

A Winter Love

I can feel cold in winter.
Cold is freezing my wet soil.
Snowflakes softly make a halo
As you watch me closer and closer.
You help me out of my coat.
Lean closer holds me tight.
Softly you kiss me, once, twice.
My face so closes to you closes enough to kiss.
I wonder if you kiss me again
To make winter cold become warm.
Forever to you.
The love, I wish

Our Leaders

To all of my leaders at my great company.

I write.

You pray

And try to remember their dreams.

I am the person,

born to be the leader.

For it is the only way.

I can manage to them to work hard

and build their dreams and lives etc.

Close to God

And away from sin.

I know now.

What you couldn't before.

An angel needs to be alive,

to appreciate our leaders

Friends –

To all poet friends

Crossing distance,
the moon hidden,
pain within my heart,
tired of working hard.
Enjoy moment with friends
calm my anxiety,
and sadness will go…
Forever of my life.

That Summer Moment

As I sit there dreaming of the morning summer so perfect-
the times you hold me so close
to see in those beautiful blue skies- the gleam of all that
dreams. . .
For the full happiness - our loves never ending
to feel the rhythm of your heart and mine,
as our hearts beat in the perfect time
to feel you and me, as if by our souls -
holding on that perfect time,
in our love captures of self to you only
That summer in time of self - me and you
forever to you
My love I give.

I dreamed...

Mom, the peace already has in Vietnam.
I love the rivers of the South Vietnam.
I love the flowers "Phu?o?ng Vi?" on the dirty roads
and I wish the democracy for Vietnam.
For the poorest people are not suffering
And the yellow moon is illuminated on the rivers.
I love the poorest people
That lives in the simple lives
with the faith loves
Of the waits of husbands or wives.

The languages

To the people who find the freedom.

If you still have the language.
You have the country, the lovers,
the dreams and the lives etc.
Yes, more and more than those. . .
Oh, my goodness!
When I think of my native country.
I feel so much pain, boring and suffering
In the control of Mr. Vietnamese President.
I also feel so much pain for boat people who need to
find their livings, the freedom, their dreams etc.
I want to pray and wish them to
reach to the land of freedom.
To help them with my Vietnamese language
Or English or French or Chinese or Spanish or India. . .
If I can help them do the best as I can.

Once again, may Lord God bless them?
And thanks so much to the best Mr. President
who gave the freedom of Iraq.
Therefore, I can use the languages to help the people.

Afternoon Autumn's Love

When we walk through the colored leaves.
Our hearts become warm.
Your love wraps me up like the great sunshine.
With you, afternoon autumn
Alive the sweet memories.
To the beautiful colored leaves
And stay in there for entire afternoon
to feel peace and true love
Coming into our souls.

When you was kissing me.
I were watching the sky of the autumn,
the dim moon under sky of the
Nature's lovely way
I thought of you as it kisses,
the whole day into evening.
With love, I will be yours forever.

The Christmas

For the Christmas's DAY

The colorful Christmas tree
with the gifts,
and the illuminated lights
hang on over the trees,
children gather around the tree
to let you know Christmas's Eve
on it's way.
They sing the songs
with all the smiles
Dancing and playing. . .

. . . That with simple wishes
of all people
Themselves to understand
that
"All is as Christmas should be"

Loving you

The yellow moon under the sky
through cloud, through stars
guiding my thoughts
To you, my honey.

My heart is beating your love
as you feel my deep emotion,
as times passed by,
to make naked
Still for you and me.

As you kiss me softly on my lips,
eyes and my face etc.
As you touch me
to undress.

My desires quietly.
We melt together one.
As my heart fills with
Full happiness of loving you.

Him and Fall

He left her that day,
the sunshine is raised.
Every fall passed by.
The bitter teardrops on her eyes,
she counts the time ran out.
Despair the hope to say good bye.
She heard the rain, the windy.
The rain holds her heart warm.
The autumn leaves fall down quietly.
The moon under dim sky of the
nature's lovely way,
She is always waiting for him.
To dream to become one.
To the fall that is crying
after her wait.

You are...

For the Valentine's DAY

I am the young girl,
he is the man
Hold me tight
to kiss me,
to touch my skin
For having feeling blue.
It is raining at Seattle.
The loneliness flies to the wind
as happy as we can be.
Count the time passed by,
you and I love each other.
Wishing our age is younger
About eighteen or twenty year olds.
It is always raining at Seattle,
So I stand close to you
to let you know
You are... my lover.

The red rose

This poem for the Valentine's Day

This is red rose
for you only.
Loving you so much
And wanting you make me
become the lover.
For only when we are together
our hearts and souls
Become one's life
brighten like the red rose.
Making the journey of
love a wonderful life.

Don't ask me

For all the poets who fall in love during autumn.

Don't ask me. . . when will the autumn begin?
For the skies are ambiguous,
for the autumn leaves fall down,
the windy is on its way.

Don't ask me. . . if I can see
The moon in the dimly lit sky,
the autumn's soul becomes lovely
And our poems will live for a thousand years

Don't ask me. . . when is it not raining in autumn?
For rain does not drop upon your lips,
and my teardrops fall from my eyes,
but my heart is not broken.
And our love will never end.

Don't ask me. . . How long before you stop thinking
of me, and I of you?

Grandma

Oh! Grandma. Where did you go?
Yet, I never got a chance to say goodbye.
You and I met every summer.
I remembered you prayed every night for the whole family.

You died long ago
But you were up in heaven gate
and waved me in the sweet
dreams of my childhood.

Grandma I love you so much.
I wish I could talk to you
To remember the hot summer
Of the harvest of grapefruits, plums, lemons etc.

Grandma- you are the best, I love you for your kindness.
I wish I went back to the best souvenirs
that we lived long ago.
Forever to you - The love I give

The morning love

This morning, when the sunshine is arising:
That warmth love's early morning is beginning,
your lovely hands hold for mine
And hold me closer and closer.

Not even realize that fall
of the last season.
The autumn leaves fall down fast
that it starts to winter chilled,
the moon under dim sky of the
nature's lovely way.
But now, dear honey, you love me.

And I let my fingers warm in your fingers
to know the morning love begin to start:
Kiss me soft to undress me,
skin to my skin, nothing held within
and in doing making love as
The morning sunshine illuminated.

Strong feeling of morning love
still exists in you and me.
Our souls will always wait for morning
love a minute and begin again.

Desire

You can't see that you made me cry.
I want you to hold me in your arms.
But I can't feel the warmth without you're here.
For I can't see you face by face.
I want to say quietly:
"I love you more than any thing else
like the sea of the Pacific,
Take my soul sink in the dream love"
If you can feel my eyes
And you can see how you're tearing me apart,
my teardrops are on my eyes
Like the raining of the late fall.
Torn between what you want and what I desire.
But now, I am falling for you.
I wish you could feel my desire.
When my eyes are no longer see you.
Then the darkness of love ends.
And I want to say:
"You are my everything
and every thing is you"
Forever, my desire will be my wish.

The lovely Fall

That afternoon I feel cold,
In the windy fall of this year.
My happiness is grown
In beginning again.
Each day I write the romantic poem
For my love in the sweet dream," missing him".
The fall is so marvelous:
The yellow moon on the dim sky,
autumn leaves fall down quietly.
The world of poems in the glass of wine
His soul drinks that glass of wine
And hold my body warm in his mind.
Like the rose is just bloomed
In the lovely fall.

Teenager

To my teenager friend's lover.
He knew her when she was teenager.
The afternoon school breaks with dating.
"Purple" of missing. . .
Kiss her neck to feel her beauty:
Her deep black eyes, her laugh, her grace,
her more than just someone to him.
As he thinks of her like the dream of life.
Now he is teenager.
He still loves her like the beginning
and dreams of her days and nights.
Together, they will be forever

Love you

Love you I sent the romantic poem.
Know you when I read your great poems.
The whole love of our wishing and
As beautiful as the roses.
Love you as the simple dream.
Love you; behold me like the dream lover.
And I have fallen for you as fast as
I will be with you, just simply love you.
Together, our love will be forever.

The kisses

You kiss, cheerful, inside of my house.
You kiss, my soul is arousing.
Sometime your kisses explode.
Near you, my life is happy.
Oh! Your kisses are so soft.
Smooth as the soul of you.
The kisses of the great person do not compare.
Your kisses are so simple.
You kiss my lips; your kisses turn me on.
No matter what the kind of the kisses, the kisses are very soft.
From inside of my house, your kisses are so wonderful.
Sending all my sadness to the winds and clouds.
I want your kisses for thousands of years.
Carrying your kisses forever to the end of the horizon!
And when you are not there with me.
I still feel your kisses, enticing as waiting and wishing.

Waiting him

I am waiting him like soil needs water.
Like the mid-night waiting the morning of the sunshine.
Like the prisoner waiting the last day out.
Like the wife waiting the husband in Iraq combat.
I am waiting him in the teardrops of my eyes.
The happiness is never coming in his own good
I am waiting him in the minute or the second of my life.
My love for him like the teenager.
Leaving the country, never know when he comes back.
Let me wait him until one hundred years,
I still wait him.

The wedding's Day

The flower's car was so marvelous.
Her wedding's ring illuminated
Under great sunshine.
Her lips full and pink as roses
He gave her the long soft kiss, the smile, the joy…
Yes, more and more
And the best of the best.
Together, they became husband and wife

Only for Him

She wrote the romantic poems
only for him.
Because the love only come once.
She takes good care of him
And only for him.
The love she gave him
with full of kisses
only for him.
The happiness
Of the first love that she had,
only for him.
The red roses that she had,
only for him.
The great smile
On her face of the great sunshine
only for him.
Her love only for him,
will be forever
And only for him.

Letter for Dad

Today is my daddy's Day.
I am looking at the altar with the sadness.
My daddy was placed in the old frame.
In the temple, I hold my daddy's
face of old dream of my childhood.
Many thanks daddy, you have given me
the life, the body and the mind.
Yes, more and more...
And the best of the best.
In my mind, daddy can't compare any one else.
Daddy, you are the best
And the best of every thing.
To the heaven gate.
Daddy will place
like an Angel,
I pray him four times
and Buddha three times.
Loving them as always.

A baby boy

That morning of the dim sunshine.

The trees were ripping off roofs of the hurricane.

I saw the beautiful lady cried in hopeless:

Yelled and screamed and etc.

To help her rescue

Her baby boy swam in the big hurricane.

Oh, my goodness!

The baby cried very noisy,

he swam to find

His prayed mom.

Luckily, God has given them

the living, the joy, the love

And the very best etc.

Yes, more and more. . . .

Together they alive.

His eyes

Are the eyes windows of mind?
His eyes are the window of mind.
He beholds me like the windy love;
I can feel the sweet teardrops
Of an amazing love.
Oh, my goodness!
I alive in the sweet dreams of the young age
And awaken me in the great sunshine of blue morning.

Missing love

I miss him when I reach his eyes.
I love him when I see his face.
I think of him when I wake up at mid-night.
And having sweet dreams each night of my life.

I wish

I want the spring of marvelous sunshine.
I want the spring blow flowers,
I want my life will bloom like the red roses
and my true friends will live forever.
I wish I will have more talents
and my friends always like me.

Love

Is love brought you to a life?

When I knew him.
I found myself the pool of flowers:
Roses tulips, orchids etc.
Awaked me in the naive thought.
Love made me write the romantic poems and the love letters.
For my mind is arousing in the sweet dreams.
Oh, my goodness!
Lord is giving me the simple love
That brings me a lot of wishes, dreams and life.

Friend

When her lover die,
Run nowhere on the road,
too dark and lonely.
Sleeping in the sweet dreams.
Waking up with his shadow,
smiling and tell her:
"Honey, wait for me,
please do not run anywhere.
Goes on with your life."

The Happiness of life

In the dream of life.
I make the money
from the hard work
and like to learn.
Of course, I solve the problems for the clients
with the happiness of life
And my true friends
to build me become
The happy person.
I ask myself:
"Oh, my goodness!
What else's?
Should I dream?"
May be the big house or the nice car.
I only want the happiness of life

Mom

Mom is my country,
Bring me here for love, education.
She would not want me behind technologies.
She feeds me lot of real food.
I worry when she get sick.
Hope she will be with me forever

Autumn at Virginia

The fall at Virginia makes me like to make the poems

She lives at Virginia, he lives at Tokyo.
Virginia's autumn leaves begin fall down.
Surprising, she lives at Virginia for a while.
But they never meet each other even once.
Watching the fall leaves, he thinks of spring.
Autumn's leaves begin fall down fast.
He is missing her lot likes the romantic spring at Tokyo.
She finds herself home sweet home at Virginia
And her lover is in her hands.
With Joy and Happiness
As she thought of the lovely fall
at Virginia
Together forever
They become one in the beautiful
Virginia's fall.

Her

He is leaving her for a while.
The half of her mind gets lost.
The remind of her mind become nice.
She was waken up in the sweet dream
And suddenly see him in that dream.
Oh, her lover!
He is there in her dream
And will take her back to normal life

Buddha

To memorialize my father died and his ash placed in the temple

If I'll die,
I only ask Buddha,
take me back
Where I was belongs
To become your follower.
Oh, Buddha!
I believe the great miracle
that you have given me
With your mankind, forgiven and faith
direct me in the perfectly way,
not so evil omens.
Many thanks Buddha,
you always exist in my life.

The bittersweet love

She left her hometown that fall.
The autumn was never come back to her.
The golden leaves cried for her.
The golden leaves fall was all over,
with covered full gray cloudy sky.
In the darkness of her bitter love life.
She was never known what was true love?
Please God,
let her forget her evil ex-husband,
always made her having bad dreams:
"With the pool bloody of unborn baby died.
She suffered in the hospital bed".
Please let her went far away from him.
For her love life live in
The full happiness of the warm spring.

The dream lover

To the beautiful Queen of France Marie-Antoinette (1754-1793).

She is beautiful under sunshine,
Likes the Orchid flowers of marvelous spring.
Never met her face but knew her true love.
Under dim moon, he found her like a fairy tale.

Love Life

This poem is the moment expressed about one loved life

The lovesick tree that you planted.
The lovesick leaves fall all over the garden.
Wonder where she is.
Dreaming that we can be together.
Pick up the lovely leaves, wishing we can be together.

Life goes on

He gave her half of his life.
The half of his life for someone else.
He keeps playing and never gets bored.
This afternoon he gets lovesick.
And just wonders where she goes.

The red tulip

This poem is my thought about
The beautiful place that I worked before

Winter is almost over.
Spring will blossom the red tulips.
The red tulips of the best days.
Walking at the Capitol Hill
of the worked day,
to wish the love life will brighten
like the red tulips.

Missing colors

The Love of my purity girl friends at High School in Vietnam

Her white long-dress
makes him like Daisy.
His blue shirt,
she loves her school.
Afraid love letters not enough
meaning of love,
He is fixing the purple pen
for missing colors.

Him

Wandering on the site wall.
Lose lover made him feel loneliness.
Stepping on the snow stormed,
feeling so bitter.
With all the black birds are flying
on the cloudy sky, windy
And never know where she goes.

Loneliness

That day I dream of:
"Staying in the heaven of love.
Living in the longest day
Of first love".
Suddenly, I wake up
With the loneliness
And sadness of love life.
I gently asked
God for the blessing
and wishing something
better than love.
Love make me
feel missing
And not feel missing
if the love is not
Existing in my life any more.

Fall

Have you ever felt the autumn season?
The naive deer's step on the colored leaves.
The colored leaves bring you to the autumn.
The autumn brings the fall that awakens.
Fall creates the loveliest scene ever.
Fall's attraction of lovers
And make your heart warmer again.
Have you ever feel to the autumn season?
The naive deer's are wandering on the colored leaves.
The colored leaves bring you to the romantic fall.
The fall of youth ages and the lovers and the great lives.

The Poets

To Americans Poets who died for freedom at Iraq.

If I am the poet,

Flying in the blue clouds.

Walking in the purple rain.

Sleeping in the sweet dreams.

Living with the best souvenirs

And finally will die

like everyone else

Without regret.

The seductive evening

He met her at the office.
Got heart-break at the beginning.
She walked away and told him:
"Darling, I could not say a word,
but you can see my heart.
Beating very strongly"
In the romantic night,
Until time passed by.
She found Mr. Right.

Spring fever

I had that spring
Where he were in the class with his friends.
I once saw him flirted me.
He changed my heart became blue heaven
and melt me like the honey.
May be we can be like marbles.
Today I see the new way to live.
I could be the person he wants to destroy;
disappear in the skies or stabbed me
Like the mashed potatoes.
Until time passed by,
I finally choose my own love life
in the happiness life:
"Live with true friends
Who care, love and sense of humor, etc."

Loneliness

To the great King of France called Napoleon.

He gave her his first love life.
Surprised she kept quiet like the stone.
He ran away home to play guitar
with the broken-heart, loneliness.
His heart melts like the teardrops.
His life was wandering in an exiled island.
Until his age reached thirty five.
He thought of her
with sadly loneliness.

Him and Sunshine

To my girlfriend who falls in love her lover.

This morning she sees him
in the sunshine.
Having the day dream,
she is staying in that sunshine.
She is asking herself:
"Oh goodness!
I hope that sunshine
always in my wish
And don't want someone steal it".
Thanks sunshine.
You're always in her heart.

In his hands

To someone who is really in love.

She missed his hands so much.
For him arouses at mid-night,
for her mind sinks in sweet dreams.
Like the earth spins around them.
In his hands,
she sees the beautiful blue skies,
with the full happiness.
Can't say word to describe her love.
His hand becomes strongly,
hold her tight.
She melts like the honey
under his hot heart,
she wants the time never pass by
and always in his hands
Of the summer hot.

Our friendship

T, after seeing you another day.
The sky has turned blue and chased the gray clouds away.

The writer has enjoyed your black eyes
and tinkle in your smile.
It made the "fool that you was" still alive.
Let us hope our love life last for many days.
Until then you have a wonderful day.

The Squirrels

That morning I saw the squirrel
wised the eyes and seemed to say:
"Good morning, ms Wandering".
His tail waved me and
Jumped into the lemon tree.
When I came home
That day to feed the squirrel,
waited for me there to say:
"Good afternoon, ms Wandering",
then disappeared in the big jungle tree.
Oh, the squirrel!
"What's the cutest animal that I loved?"
I found myself the missing love
In the beautiful nature of Ohio.
I still watch fall season
That was someone else's fall.
The gray squirrels were dancing,
the ground was covered full golden leaves.
I dream of blue heaven

And traveling through Asia.

My Childhood

For the best time that I had when my parents were still alive-

My childhood
Is the long way in the pass?
With the best souvenirs that I never forget.
The memory of the innocent time,
never know what love is.
In the small world of friendship
and the parent's loves.
Oh, my childhood!
I wish I went back to the childhood
to live with best time.
Without worry the money, work.

DAD

Dad is in my sweet dream.
I remember him every day
For taking good care of me.
When missing him,
I see him at the altar
and wishing him
To have the best life
in the best country.
I love you, Dad.
You always exist in my life.

The Lady Moon

When I was born a tiny baby,
my kindness mom holds me in her arms,
felt warm like the sunshine
Which God give me
the wonderful life.
I saw Lady Moon once each year.
Oh, My Lady Moon!
"She is the most beautiful lady who
gives me my love life."
Lady Moon and Buddha
related to me a lot.
If I'll die,
I only want to
Become the follower of Buddha.
So I won't see
World changed due to weather
or the deaths of war.

Unknown heroes

To dedicate the unknown soldiers who died for freedom of Iraq

I am normal woman,
live in the sweet dreams
of the youth ages.
I love my country and true friends
who bring the peace to me,
as well as the world.
Oh, my Goodness!
"My true friends were so perfectly:
Smarts, handsomest, courage's and bravery etc. . .
Saved lot of people's lives
Without say the words".
Many thanks God!
You created the unknown heroes for the America
Victories.
Oh, my Goodness!
Once again,
May Lord God Bless America!

Thich Ca Buddha

To the temple where my father's ashes
were placed with my love for him

Thich Ca Buddha was the prince of northern India.
To become the Buddha, the Awakened One.
He left his wife and child.
To set off to seat at the feet of
the great religious teachers.
To bring people far away from human suffering.
To change people's lives:
Old and sick but still happy and peaceful.
The miracle of him makes me admire,
Thich Ca Buddha likes best picture of mine.
In the end, even he's dead.
But 2500 years later,
His teachings still help humans.
Had the Editor's choice Award of year 2005

The high school

To remember all of my friends and my Catholic teacher in Viet Nam

I missed my Gia Long high school
With my true friends in the white long-dress.
Waved me in the old dream
Of my childhood.
Time passed by fast,
It reminds me the best souvenir
that I never forget.
Oh my goodness!
I want my youth age back.
It was so wonderful
With the great Catholic teacher
who tutored me:
Studied,
had fun,
loved parents,
loved country,
read the books
and lot of
Stories of different cultures.

Had The Editor's Choice's Award of year 2005

The heroes

*This poem is for The Veterans Day
and my brother who died for freedom*

Having no meaning of that night.
Let my mind forget in the sweet dream:
"I loved my country and friend
Who sacrificed for freedom?
In that dream,
God let me wish,
They all went to heaven.
Of course, they are
The heroes."
Oh, my Goodness!
Once again,
May Lord God Bless America!

www.ingramcontent.com/pod-product-compliance
Lightning Source LLC
LaVergne TN
LVHW020435080526
838202LV00055B/5196